Companion Guide

for

The Inefficiency Assassin:
Time Management Tactics for
Working Smarter, Not Longer

D1608986

by

Helene Segura, MA Ed, CPO®

Hacienda Oaks Press

1140 S. Laredo St., Suite 830852
San Antonio, TX 78283

The Inefficiency Assassin: Time Management Tactics for Working Smarter, Not Longer is published by New
World Library. www.NewWorldLibrary.com

ISBN-13: 978-0692652718

ISBN-10: 069265271X

Hacienda Oaks Press graphic by Foster Creative

Your Time Management Revolution Starts Here!

This companion book is designed to be used for capturing notes, thoughts and lessons learned during my workshops and webinars, and while reading my book *The Inefficiency Assassin: Time Management Tactics for Working Smarter, Not Longer* (New World Library).

Each chapter has ample blank space for your notes.

As I mention in my book and trainings, I would love to tell you that I can wave a magic wand and your life will change for the better overnight, but I'm sure you know by now that that just isn't the case. Some of you may try to revolutionize everything at once, and that will work for you. Others might try implementing just one change per week or month because that's more at your comfort level.

> To get through the hardest journey we need take only one step at a time, but we must keep on stepping.
>
> Chinese Proverb

No matter how you proceed, please realize that nothing will change if you don't do something *different*.

Are you tired of feeling overwhelmed from having so much to do?

Do you want to never miss another special moment?

Do you wish you had more time in the day?

Do you want to learn how to improve productivity, so that you can increase success and decrease stress levels?

If you answered yes to any of these questions, you're in the right place.

Welcome aboard! It's time to go on a mission . . .

Background Check: What's Your Cover?

What were you like as a kid?

What are you like now as an adult?

What are your hobbies, passions, and/or interests?

What do you do for a living?

What led you to decide to start your own business or take the job you currently hold?

Do you see anything from your past and/or anything from your interests and hobbies which ties in with what you do now?

What hobbies, passions, or interests do you wish you had more time for?

What are your accomplishments?

Were the accomplishments you listed all personal or all business, or was it a combination?

What's on your bucket list?

What is your definition of a great life?

Based on your definition, do you have a great life? If your answer is "Yes," kick up your heels and give yourself a high five! If your answer is "Not yet," how close are you to it?

Part 1 - Create Clarity

Mind Management Is the Key to Time Management

.

Chapter 1

It's All in Your Head: End the Overwhelm by Adjusting Your Mindset

In this first part of the book, we'll complete exercises related to the **C** in CIA - **C**reate Clarity. You'll learn how you can care for and utilize your secret weapon, your brain.

In order to Create Clarity, we must:

Capture our priorities

Identify our targets

Administer self-care

Reflect with power

Be open to change

When you achieve this part of the mission, it makes completing the rest of the productivity operation – parts 2 and 3 - that much easier.

Capture Your Priorities

Chapter 2

Notes/Thoughts

People

_____

_____

_____

_____

_____

_____

Activities

_____

_____

_____

_____

_____

_____

Work

_____

_____

_____

_____

_____

_____

My Priorities

Personal

1 _____

2 _____

3 _____

4 _____

Work

1 _____

2 _____

3 _____

4 _____

Where will you post your personal priorities list?

Where will you post your work priorities list?

When, each day (or evening), will you view these lists?

Viewing your priorities lists on a daily basis has most likely not been a tactic you've applied regularly. How will you remind yourself to do this every day?

Where can you store these lists so that they're available for you to view when you need to make a decision?

How will implementing the strategies and tactics in this chapter benefit you?

Chapter 3

Identify Your Targets

Notes/Thoughts

Personal Priority #1: _____

What kind of outcomes related to this priority could be measured?

Personal Priority #2: _____

What kind of outcomes related to this priority could be measured?

Personal Priority #3: _____

What kind of outcomes related to this priority could be measured?

Work Priority #1: _____

What kind of outcomes related to this priority could be measured?

Work Priority #2: _____

What kind of outcomes related to this priority could be measured?

Work Priority #3: _____

What kind of outcomes related to this priority could be measured?

My Targets

Personal

1 _____

2 _____

3 _____

Work

1 _____

2 _____

3 _____

Where will you post your personal targets list?

Where will you post your work targets list?

When, each day (or evening), will you view these lists?

Viewing your targets lists on a daily basis has most likely not been a tactic you've applied regularly. How will you remind yourself to do this every day?

Where can you store these lists so that they're available for you to view when you need to make a decision?

How will implementing the strategies and tactics in this chapter benefit you?

Chapter 4

Notes/Thoughts

Administer Self-Care

What elements of self-care are you already practicing?

Which element of self-care would you like to add to what you already do?

How will you make sure it gets implemented?

How will implanting the strategies and tactics in this chapter benefit you?

Reflect with Power

Chapter 5

Notes/Thoughts

On what day(s) each week will you have your power reflection?

Where will this reflection take place?

What reminder will you set for yourself to make sure it happens?

How will implanting the strategies and tactics in this chapter benefit you?

Rendezvous: Your Date with Change...and Discomfort

Chapter 6

Notes/Thoughts

Do you feel any discomfort from trying to change?

If so, how will you work through it?

What will your reward be for getting through the change?

Part 2 – Implement Structure *and* Flow

Support Your Time Management Revolution by Controlling These Five Key Elements of Your Workday

Chapter 7

It's All in Your Head:
Prevent Drowning through Structure
and Flow

In order to be an agent of change in our Time Management Revolution, we must **I**mplement Structure *and* Flow. We must be able to control, yet also modify, these five key components of our workday:

A

G

E

N

T

When you achieve the first part of the mission, **C**reate Clarity (part 1), it makes completing this portion of your Time Management Revolution that much easier.

Manage Long-Term Projects with Mega-Efficiency

Chapter 8

Notes/Thoughts

What are your goals for the project?

_____

_____

_____

_____

What steps will you need to take to get there?

_____

_____

_____

_____

_____

_____

_____

_____

_____

_____

_____

_____

_____

_____

What materials and resources will you need for each step?

_____

_____

_____

_____

Who all will need to be involved with each step?

_____

_____

_____

_____

How much time will each of these steps take?

(List here or add to what you listed above.)

_____

_____

_____

_____

_____

_____

_____

_____

How has not using a detailed timeline affected you?

How will creating a timeline for your long-term projects help you?

You probably already have deadlines set for various projects. Have you already completed task timelines for each one and scheduled time blocks into your calendar? If not, which project will you start with in creating a timeline?

Chapter 9

Get It All Done in 24 Hours:
Turn To-Do Lists into *Done* Lists!

Notes/Thoughts

When will you determine your 3+3 for the next day?

Do you currently use only one long task list, or do you pull a few tasks out from there to work on each day?

What aspects of your current system are working or not working for you?

Based on what you've just learned, what changes will you make and why?

Chapter 10

Set Reminders, and Never Forget Again!

Notes/Thoughts

What effect do you think implementing a Mind Liberation will have on you?

When each day will you complete this Mind Liberation?

What capture mechanism will you use for your daily/nightly Mind Liberation?

Would you prefer that this be a free-for-all capture without structure, or do you want your ideas placed into categories (work/home, this week/next week/next month, etc.)?

How will you remind yourself to do this?

Speaking of reminders, what reminder system(s) are you already using?

Are they working? Why or why not?

If they're not working as well as you'd like, what checks-and-balances systems can you put in place, making it darn near impossible to forget anything?

If you fear forgetting to do something, what can you do to push past that thought and move forward?

How will you remind yourself to not let second-guessing get in your way?

How will implementing the strategies and tactics in this chapter benefit you?

Chapter 11

Set Up and Maintain a Productive Work Space

Notes/Thoughts

What about your current office is working for you? Why?

What about your current office is not working for you? Why?

Based on what you've just learned, what types of adjustments will you need to make?

What zones will you need to create in your office?

Will you be able to make these changes in one full day of rearranging or in a weekend, or will you need to work 30 minutes a day on different sections until the project is completed?

Dig Out from a Buried Office

Chapter 12

Notes/Thoughts

When will you set aside time to plan?

Will you need to sort in your office space, or can you pull things out a little at a time to a separate area?

What boxes or containers can you use to set up the various categories you'll divide items into?

Where can you set up all of the above boxes, so that you create a mini "store" for your categories of items?

Where can you take the shredding?

Where can you take the recycling?

Where can you take the trash?

Where can you take the donations?

Based on what you've just learned, what kind of pace and timeline do you want to schedule for yourself?

What motivation and/or accountability partner will you use to make sure that you finish this project?

Create a Go-Bag and Mobile Office for Road Warriors

Notes/Thoughts

What about your current mobile office is working for you? Why?

What about your current mobile office is not working for you? Why?

Based on what you've just read, what types of adjustments will you need to make?

What compartments will you need to create in your go-bag and/or mobile office?

Will you be able to make these changes in one full day of rearranging or a weekend, or will you need to work 30 minutes a day on different sections?

Chapter 14

Set Boundaries in the Digital Age

Notes/Thoughts

Are you going to be the boss of your time, or are you going to let some computer or phone own you?

When will you turn off your notifications?

What schedule will you set for emailing, texting, and checking/posting on social media?

On the home screens of your devices, are there any apps that tempt you?

If so, when will you move them to the rear or remove them from your device?

How will implementing the strategies and tactics in this chapter benefit you?

Chapter 15

Manage Your Incoming Email

Notes/Thoughts

Do you control your email, or does your email control you?

What is one email tactic discussed that you already use and will continue to do so because it saves you time?

What is one new email tactic that you will begin implementing today in order to save more time?

What types of templates might save you time?

What will those templates need to say?

How will implementing the strategies and tactics in this chapter benefit you?

Dig Out from a Flooded Inbox

Notes/Thoughts

How many emails do you have in your inbox?

What maximum number of emails in your Inbox would you be comfortable with?

What timeline will you use to complete this project?

Utilize the Telephone More Efficiently

Notes/Thoughts

Do you unnecessarily spend time on the phone?

If so, what do you think is causing this?

Which of the tactics are you already implementing?

Which of the tactics will you start implementing?

How long can you go without answering your phone?

What will your voicemail greeting state?

Chapter 18

Set up a Simple Filing System That Works

Notes/Thoughts

What is working with your current system that you should continue implementing?

What is bothering you about your current filing structure?

What types of papers do you need to retrieve on a daily, weekly, monthly, quarterly or yearly basis?

Determine the categories of papers you receive and retrieve.

What types of storage containers will work best for your situation?

What are the best locations for these storage containers?

How will implementing the strategies and tactics in this chapter benefit you?

Chapter 19

Deal with Incoming Daily Paper

Notes/Thoughts

How often do you currently process your papers?

In what state are your papers as a result of your current processing schedule?

How would you like things to be different?

At what time each day will you **DID** your papers?

If you've got a large stack of papers waiting for your attention, what timeline will you use to **DID** them?

Chapter 20

Take Notes Anytime, Anywhere and Never Lose Them

Notes/Thoughts

How much time do you spend looking for notes?

What capture method are you currently using?

What about it is working or not working for you?

What processing method are you currently using?

What about it is working or not working for you?

What filing method are you currently using?

What about it is working or not working for you?

What changes will you make to improve your situation?

Chapter 21

Know Where Your Time Goes, So That You Can Tell Your Time What to Do

Notes/Thoughts

Helene Segura
Kick chaos to the curb!

The T.E.A.C.H. Approach™ Week Planner

	Monday	Tuesday	Wednesday	Thursday	Friday
Theme					
5:00 AM					
5:30					
6:00					
6:30					
7:00					
7:30					
8:00					
8:30					
9:00					
9:30					
10:00					
10:30					
11:00					
11:30					
12:00 PM					
12:30					
1:00					
1:30					
2:00					
2:30					
3:00					
3:30					
4:00					
4:30					

Helene Segura
Kick chaos to the curb!

The T.E.A.C.H. Approach™ Week Planner

Theme	Monday	Tuesday	Wednesday	Thursday	Friday
5:00 PM					
5:30					
6:00					
6:30					
7:00					
7:30					
8:00					
8:30					
9:00					
9:30					
10:00					
10:30					
11:00					
11:30					
12:00 AM					
12:30					
1:00					
1:30					
2:00					
2:30					
3:00					
3:30					
4:00					
4:30					

What's your biggest a-ha from tracking your time?

There are probably some traitorous time leaks sabotaging your days...a little here and a little there. Where are you losing time?

What can you do differently to prevent that time from being lost?

Chapter 22

Schedule Around Your Personal Priorities and Targets

Notes/Thoughts

Personal Tasks

	Monday	Tuesday	Wednesday	Thursday	Friday
Theme					
5:00 AM					
5:30					
6:00					
6:30					
7:00					
7:30					
8:00					
8:30					
9:00					
9:30					
10:00					
10:30					
11:00					
11:30					
12:00 PM					
12:30					
1:00					
1:30					
2:00					
2:30					
3:00					
3:30					
4:00					
4:30					

Helene Segura
Kick chaos to the curb!

The T.E.A.C.H. Approach™ Week Planner

www.HeleneSegura.com

	Monday	Tuesday	Wednesday	Thursday	Friday
Theme					
5:00 PM					
5:30					
6:00					
6:30					
7:00					
7:30					
8:00					
8:30					
9:00					
9:30					
10:00					
10:30					
11:00					
11:30					
12:00 AM					
12:30					
1:00					
1:30					
2:00					
2:30					
3:00					
3:30					
4:00					
4:30					

83

How does the draft you just created differ from what you're currently doing?

Which of the personal tasks you listed could possibly be completed by someone else?

How will viewing your priorities and targets on a daily basis help support the strategies and tactics in this chapter for protecting your time?

How does it feel knowing that you're on your way to building a schedule that supports your work yet allows you to have a life outside of it?

Chapter 23

Determine Your High-Value Work Responsibilities

Notes/Thoughts

Work Tasks

Tasks: I must do

Tasks: Maybe I, or maybe someone else could do

Tasks: Someone else definitely could do

Tasks: Does this really need to be done?

What are your highest-value work tasks? In other words, what are the three tasks that bring your company the most money (or customers or high ratings, etc.) that no one else – only you can do?

You just determined what your high value tasks are. How much time have you been spending on these?

Which of the work tasks you listed could possibly be completed by someone else?

Can any tasks be dropped because they're of little to no value?

How does it feel knowing that you're on your way to building a schedule that supports your work yet allows you to have a life outside of it?

Schedule Around Your Work Priorities and Targets

Notes/Thoughts

How does the draft you just created differ from what you're currently doing?

How will viewing your priorities and targets on a daily basis help support the strategies and tactics for protecting your time?

What time blocks from your current draft do you need to be prepared for flip-flopping around?

What will you do to stay focused on your high-value tasks, instead of choosing to allow low-value tasks to creep into and take over – sabotage - your day?

Chapter 25

Scheduling for Road Warriors

Notes/Thoughts

How are your road warrior days currently scheduled?

Which tactics from this chapter are you already implementing and you will keep doing so?

Which tactics from this chapter will you add to your tool bag to help you improve your efficiency?

If your job takes you out of town, how will you modify the strategies and tactics in this chapter to be successful on the road and have time to catch up and regroup when you get back home?

Part 3 - Assemble Your Team

Life and Work Are Not Solo Missions

Chapter 26

It's All in Your Head:

It Takes a Village

If you're applying what you learned in the **C** of CIA – **C**reate Clarity – your mind is freeing up space to allow your brain to make better decisions about how you use your time.

If you're applying what you learned in the **I** of CIA – **I**mplement Structure *and* Flow – you're applying the strategies and tactics that will allow you to control the five key components of your workday and tell your time what to do.

In this part, we'll examine the **A** in CIA – **A**ssemble Your Team.

You'll learn how to:

 structure your personal team

 structure your work team

 communicate and interact with your team

Chapter 27

Assemble Your Personal Team

Notes/Thoughts

Who will be on your personal team?

What support do you want from them?

What support will you give to them?

How often will you meet?

How will implementing the strategies and tactics in this chapter benefit you?

Assemble Your Work Team

Would you prefer to meet with your team in person, or are you comfortable with Skype or FaceTime? (This helps you narrow down the geographic location of your team members.)

At this point in time, what kind of support do you need?

Who in your industry would be ideal for your work team?

Who outside of your industry would be ideal for your work team?

Who within your company would be ideal for your work team?

When and where would you be able to meet with your team(s)?

How will implementing the strategies and tactics in this chapter benefit you?

Facilitate Productive Team Meetings

Chapter 29

Notes/Thoughts

Are there any meetings that are a waste of your time that you should no longer attend?

If you are absolutely required to attend the above meetings, how can you make them more beneficial to yourself and everyone else there?

How much time do you lose each week to coworkers, employees, or contractors interrupting you with questions or requests to help with their "emergencies"?

What type of agenda would you like to have at your work team meetings?

What type of agenda would you like to have at your personal team meetings?

Chapter 30

Delegate the Right Stuff to the Right People

Notes/Thoughts

How much time will you be able to save by removing unnecessary tasks from your life?

How much time will you be able to save by delegating necessary but low-value tasks to others?

Once you have the job description and characteristics hashed out, do you want to go through the hiring process on your own, or should you contract out to a company to do this for you?

Keeping in mind that it can take several weeks to develop a job description, many more weeks to hire, and usually one to two months to train, what type of realistic timeline would you like to set for your hiring needs?

If you work for a company, how will you apply the tactics from this chapter to help your colleagues restructure tasks and work more efficiently together on projects?

Instead of, or in addition to, the previous question, how will you apply the tactics from this chapter to create a hiring proposal for your supervisor?

Part 4

Situational Solutions

Chapter 31

I Multitask, but I Still Can't Finish Everything

Notes/Thoughts

If you multitask or task-switch, what are the common causes?

How long is your attention span?

When is your best brain time?

Where is your most productive work area?

What steps will you take to cut back on multitasking and task-switching?

How will implementing the strategies and tactics in this chapter benefit you?

Chapter 32

My Brain Is Constantly in Overdrive

Notes/Thoughts

What are your work hours?

What are your possible work/break times?

When is your first possible play day (or half-day)?

What are some nonbusiness conversation topics you can have on standby?

What are some possible future nonwork obsessions?

How will implementing the strategies and tactics in this chapter benefit you?

Chapter 33

I've Got Brainus Interruptus and Ideas Overload

Notes/Thoughts

How often do random thoughts or ideas interrupt your train of thought?

Often we stay on autopilot and don't realize that we've completely switched tasks and are now working on that new thought or idea. How will you recognize that this interruption is occurring?

What capture mechanism will you use for your brainus interruptus deflector shield?

How will implementing the strategies and tactics in this chapter benefit you?

Chapter 34

I Am Constantly Interrupted or Distracted

Notes/Thoughts

How much time can you gain back daily just by cutting down on interruptions?

How does allowing constant interruptions support your progress toward your priorities and targets? (That's right! It's a trick question!)

What constitutes a true emergency at home? (Think life or death.)

What constitutes a true emergency at work? (Think life or death for your job.)

If someone tells you that this focused-work stuff is stupid, what is something you can say to get him or her out of your hair?

Chapter 35

When Crap Happens, I Go Into a Tailspin

Notes/Thoughts

To help you keep things in perspective when bad stuff happens, what do you consider annoying versus catastrophic?

In the event that something catastrophic happens, who in your life is patient and wise and would be willing to help you brainstorm?

Who/what are positive people/things in your life? What positivity can you focus on in the event of a disaster?

How will implementing the strategies and tactics in this chapter benefit you?

Chapter 36

I Procrastinate...A Lot

Notes/Thoughts

If you procrastinate, what are the common causes?

What does it feel like when you're about to procrastinate?

When you catch yourself feeling that way, what steps will you take to cut back on procrastination?

How much time will you save each day by cutting back on procrastination?

Chapter 37

I May Not Be a Perfectionist, but I Want Everything Just Right

Notes/Thoughts

How much time do you think perfectionism costs you?

What would you rather do with that time?

If you fear not perfectly completing a recommendation from the book, training or webinar, what can you do to push past that thought and complete the recommendation?

How will you remind yourself to not let perfectionism get in the way of what you want to accomplish?

Chapter 38

I Have a Tough Time Sleeping

Notes/Thoughts

How has a lack of sleep affected you?

When will you complete your Mind Liberation?

What will you do to stop drinking nonwater liquids and eating at least two hours before bedtime?

How will you remember to turn off your electronics a minimum of 30 minutes before bedtime?

What will you do for relaxation during those (minimum) 30 minutes?

Chapter 39

I'm Often Late or Miss Appointments

Notes/Thoughts

How often are you late to appointments?

What do you think is causing this?

How often do you miss appointments completely?

What do you think is causing this?

Based on what you've just learned, which strategies and tactics will you apply in order to be on time to all future appointments?

If anyone – including the devil (or boogieman) on your shoulder – ever gives you a hard time about implementing any of the tactics in this checks and balances system, what response can you have ready that explains how this is helpful to you?

Chapter 40

I Often Let Great Opportunities Turn into Big Stress

Notes/Thoughts

What strategies and tactics from this chapter do you already use, and what is it about them that works for you?

How will implementing the strategies and tactics in this chapter prevent you from getting overloaded?

It's important to have responses ready to go – on automatic – when you are approached by someone and asked to take on a task or project. What are three different responses you can use to delay an answer to a request?

What if they say they need an answer immediately? What are three responses you can have ready to give to delay them at least 10 minutes – long enough for you to go through the steps in this chapter at a rapid rate?

What if you aren't given the chance to say no or set a deadline? What are some negotiating tactics you can have ready in your back pocket should the need arise?

When can you rehearse these responses and tactics so that you don't forget them in a panic if an intimidating customer or your boss snarls at you?

Chapter 41

I Have to Drop Everything When My Clients Call Me in Crisis

Notes/Thoughts

How much time can you gain back weekly or monthly just by cutting down on fighting fires for your client emergencies?

How does allowing these types of interruptions support your progress toward your work priorities and targets? (That's right! It's a trick question!)

What constitutes a true emergency for a client? (Think life or death for your business or the company for which you work.)

Which of these emergencies, if any, are you willing to assist with?

Which of these emergencies, if any, will be a part of your standard services, and which will require additional contracts?

Whether you work for a company or own your own business, what preventive measures could be in place to help your customers avoid crises?

Chapter 42

I'd Love to Control My Time, but I Don't Know What to Say to People

Notes/Thoughts

Which of these tactics are you already applying successfully?

What words or actions have you used in the past that have not been successful?

What will you do differently to protect your time?

Using the templates as a guide, what phrases can you have ready to go for situations that crop up frequently for you?

When will you rehearse these lines?

Chapter 43

I Never Stick to My Time Management Plan

Notes/Thoughts

You may be familiar with many of the strategies and tactics discussed in the book, trainings or webinars, but how many have you applied on a regular basis?

Which strategies and tactics have you not been using, which could be why you haven't been sticking to your time management plan?

How determined are you to improve your time management and productivity?

If any success-blocking vocabulary enters your brain, how will you eliminate it?

Conclusion

Be an Agent of Change in Your Time Management Revolution

You will be productive *and* have a life outside of your business or your job.

You will work smarter, not longer.

Productivity.

Balance.

Happiness.

Success.

Peace.

Time management is all about mind-set and *mind* management.

It truly is...all in your head.

The End.

Resources and Intel

If you wander over to www.HeleneSegura.com/30tactics, you'll find links to time management planning templates, research by neuroscientists and psychologists that supports what I recommend, a glossary, apps and software programs that might be useful tools, suggestions of helpful office supplies and great books, quote sources, videos, and more.

About the Author

The author of two Amazon bestselling books, Helene Segura has been the featured productivity expert in more than 100 media interviews, in publications such as *U.S. News and World Report* and *Money Magazine,* as well as on Fox, CBS, ABC, and NBC affiliates. Born and raised in Los Angeles, she earned her bachelor's degree from Texas A&M University (Gig 'em!) and her master's degree from the University of Texas at San Antonio.

By day, Helene presents keynotes and trainings as The Inefficiency Assassin™ and teaches audiences and clients how to slay wasted time. By night (and on weekends), she's a devout cheese eater, a recipe experimenter, and a travel junkie. If you blink, you might miss her sneaking adult beverages onto the lawn bowling court.

For information about keynotes, workshops, books, webinars, and individual coaching, or to connect with Helene via social media (you're on the honor system not to procrastinate!), visit www.HeleneSegura.com.

Photo by Korey Howell